snowmen

snowmen

SNOW CREATURES, CRAFTS, AND OTHER WINTER PROJECTS

 BY peter cole,
frankie frankeny,
and leslie jonath

PHOTOGRAPHS BY
frankie frankeny

CHRONICLE BOOKS

SAN FRANCISCO

Text copyright © 1999 by Peter Cole, Frankie Frankeny, and
    Leslie Jonath.
Photography copyright © 1999 by Frankie Frankeny.

Library of Congress Cataloging-in-Publication Data:
Frankeny, Frankie.
    Snowmen : snow creatures, crafts, and other winter projects/
by Frankie Frankeny, Peter Cole, and Leslie Jonath.
        p. cm.
        ISBN 0-8118-2554-X (hc)
        1. Handicraft 2. Snow sculpture 3. Snowmen
        I. Cole, Peter. II. Jonath, Leslie, 1964- . III. Title.
    TT149.F73 1999
    745.5—dc21   99-20145
                          CIP

Manufactured in China.

Food styling by Wesley Martin.
Designed and typeset by Anne Galperin.

Distributed in Canada by Raincoast Books
8680 Cambie Street
Vancouver, British Columbia V6P 6M9

10 9 8 7 6 5 4 3 2

Chronicle Books
85 Second Street
San Francisco, California 94105

www.chroniclebooks.com

For their creative ideas and snow-building brawn, we'd like to thank Wesley Martin, Anna Loring, and Alison Richman. Special thanks to Wesley for his original recipes and stellar food styling.

ACKNOWLEDGMENTS

We'd also like to thank our fabulous editor, Mikyla Bruder, designer Anne Galperin, and production coordinator Shona Bayley, as well as Julianne Balmain, Sharon Silva, Elise Cannon, Stephanie Rosenbaum, Jisho Warner, Sara Schneider, Dean Burrell, Julie Glantz, Susan Greenwood, Andrea Hirsh, Jessica Strand, Jennifer Vetter, and Tera Killip for their invaluable contributions.

c✳ntents

WHO WOULD HAVE THOUGHT that snow, the precipitation of small white ice crystals formed directly from the water vapor of the air at a temperature of less than thirty-two degrees, could

intr✻DUCTION

inspire such feats of artistry? The exact origins of the snow-man remain mysterious, but it seems that people were making snow figures before they could say "pack and roll." What we do know is that the word *snow* has been used by English speakers since the beginning of the tenth century, and used to describe the dark, transient spots on a television screen for over two decades. The Eskimos were once thought to have more than one hundred words for snow. (As it turns out, this isn't entirely true.) Glaciology is the branch of science devoted to snow.

ALL OVER THE WORLD, people have turned bad weather into great sculpture—from the igloos of Alaska to the Ice Palace in Finland, from the *Bonhommes*

de Neiges of France to the mega-snowman of Bethel, Maine. If you've got snow, chances are you've got snowmen. Snowmen are hip, they're trendy, you could even say they're cool.

BUT MAKING SNOWMEN IS not just about making a three-tiered homage to the Michelin man. Snow is a great medium, a brilliant white three-dimensional canvas with infinite sculpting possibilities. And it's free! With a few tools and some physical exertion, you can create a winter won-derland full of creatures and buildings, planets, movie stars, and more—from the simple to the spectacular, from the sub-lime to the superbly ridiculous.

BEFORE YOU START, GET to know your snow. Take inspiration from your landscape. Look carefully at the natural mounds, drifts, and snow-banks. Are there huge lumps that cry out to be a Kon Tiki or a woolly mammoth? Are there stoic banks and bluffs that say "Grand Canyon" or moguls that hint at the outlines of sea turtles or VW Bugs? Like finding shapes in the clouds, you can find inspiration in what's already there.

SNOW SCULPTING IS ONLY the beginning. Once you create the basic form, it's time to prop until you drop. In snowmen, we have used simple everyday objects to bring the snow figures to life: pot lids, funky clothes, fabric scraps, fruits and vegetables, pinecones and branches. Borrow ideas from your favorite artists! Just remember to retrieve your stuff before there's a meltdown and the family jewels float out to sea. (Make art, not litter.)

MOST OF THE SCULPTURES in this book can be completed with a minimum of equipment and technical grace. We have included a few large projects, however, that require more time and extra hands. You might want to start with a smaller project to get the feel of working with snow. The Snow Bunnies (see page 37), for example, take only a half-hour to create. Once you've mastered

the basic techniques, build Snowby Dick (see page 44), an enormous endeavor that makes a wondrous, athletic all-day event. Of course, all the dimensions we cite are rough guidelines. You can scale down a project or make it even larger. Building with snow is a great opportunity to spend quality time with family and friends or a terrific excuse to meet the neighbors. (Who knows? They might let you drive their snowblower!)

JUST AS NO TWO snowflakes are alike, no two snowmen will ever be the same. If your snowman won't fit in the freezer, keep the memory alive with a photograph. An album documents what you build each season and how long each project lasts. You might want to hold your own winter carnival and create an annual snow-sculpting tradition.

SO GO PLAY IN the snow! Just make sure to wear warm, waterproof clothes (especially gloves), and remember to take time out for lunch.

9

working with snow

AS ANY SNOW SURVEYOR will tell you, snow comes in many conditions. Generally, fresh wet snow is easier to pack and mold, while older firm snow is easier to sculpt. Most structures can be built with any type of snow using variations of these simple techniques. Listed here are the basic techniques favored by our team of snow fanatics. Of course, you may have your own time-tested ways.

massing

To make a large mass, gather up snow, packing from the ground up in the shape of a volcano. When massing tall structures, start by building a wider base than you need. It is easier to overbuild the initial form and carve it down to size.

packing

Wet snow is the easiest snow to pack. Grainy, icy, or dry snow will stick to itself better if you first dampen it using a spray bottle filled with water. You can build structures by stacking rough blocks of old snow, filling the crevices with powder, and spraying. The water spray freezes, thus holding the shape. Continue packing and then spraying until you have the desired mass. Hard packed snow is easiest to carve.

carving

Start by carving the rough shape for any snow figure before moving to the details. Flat, broad garden trowels and spades are good for carving the larger forms; serrated edges are best for honing finer details. Carving tools don't have to be sharp. Instead of using a handsaw to cut blocks from a snowbank, use a rimless cookie sheet to slice through the snow. Employ metal spoons and blunt butter knives to scoop out holes for eyes and to carve other features. Use shovels to carve broad deep undercuts around the base of any figure for shadow and definition.

MOLDING

Make snow blocks by pressing wet snow (like cookie dough) into smooth-sided containers such as metal baking pans, mixing bowls, plastic storage containers, plastic cups, or Jell-O molds. Dry snow or powder doesn't mold very well, but it can be moistened using a spray bottle filled with water. Once you have pressed all the snow tightly into molds, unmold by turning the molds upside down to free the shape. The blocks can then be stacked in various ways to build larger and more intricate forms.

ROLLING

Rolling the perfect snowball goes beyond technique into the realm of instinct. The experts we consulted recommended the pack-and-roll method. Pack a ball of fresh wet snow in your palms, roll it once or twice on the ground, and pack again. Continue rolling and packing until the ball reaches the desired size.

STAKING

Wooden stakes are useful for reinforcing or for adding to a large structure. Build outstretched arms on a figure by carefully packing snow around stakes stuck at right angles into the body or use stakes to hold heads, hats, legs, and any other appendages needing extra support, especially on windy days or on steeper inclines. Wooden skewers work well for lighter additions.

FRAMING

Although most of the structures in this book were built without them, frames are useful for more intricate forms. We used pine boards and $2\frac{1}{2}$-inch screws to construct Rudolph's skeleton (see page 19). Before packing snow up around a wood frame, wet the wood using a spray bottle filled with water. The snow will stick better.

HeLPFUL TOOLS

snow shovels, garden shovels, and spades for massing, moving, mounding, and digging

rimless cookie sheets for carving and cutting large snow bricks

metal spatulas and garden trowels for scraping and cutting corners and edges

spoons and butter knives for scooping, carving, and smoothing

serrated knives for shaving and detailed carving (keep away from children!)

plastic, metal, and other nonstick containers for molding

spray bottles filled with water for wetting snow

garden shears for cutting sticks and making pegs

kitchen lighter with an extended handle for lighting candles

plastic garbage cans for building large structures

baling or other sturdy, pliable wire for joining branches and attaching decorations

hammers for driving stakes

wooden toothpicks and skewers for attaching decorations

wire cutters for cutting wire

pliers for twisting wire

screwdriver for making frames and drilling small holes

handsaw for cutting wood frames and snow bricks

Decorating

DECORATING IS THE FUN part. What you choose to use is limited only by your creativity and physical reality. Smooth plastic props don't stick well to snow. It's best to use textured objects, especially natural materials—fallen branches, pine needles and pine cones, icicles, rocks—that are readily available and environmentally friendly. You might also find inspiration from the items in your garden, kitchen, garage, and closets. We scavenged most of our materials from such places. Hardware, craft, or art-supply stores are great resources for other fun stuff.

Most decorations can be attached by burrowing them directly into the figure. If the snow is hard or your decorations unruly, peg them with toothpicks or wooden skewers. (Those shish kabob skewers in the supermarket have a million great uses.)

Ideas for Decorations

natural materials such as pinecones, pine needles, rocks, fallen branches, sticks, berries, icicles

fabric (felt sticks to snow like Velcro)

ribbons, barrettes, wigs, hats, coats

spools, buttons

old hats, gloves, scarves

bright, colorful produce such as apples, carrots, eggplants, apples, broccoli, beans, oranges

bottle caps, pots and pans (and lids), colanders, whisks

nontoxic dry tempera paints for coloring snow

CHAPTER ONE

no people like
snow people

BUILD FROSTY AS BIG as a house. The secret to his size lies in massing his base over a trash can. We gave our big guy boxing gloves instead of mittens. Now he's the greatest!

seven-foot frosty

30-gallon plastic garbage can

shovel

spray bottle filled with water

1 wooden stake, approximately
  2 feet long

spoon

2 lumps of coal

wooden skewers

1 carrot

toothpicks, if using curved twig

small curved twig or
  6 medium-sized rocks

pipe (preferably corncob)

1 or more scarves

3 large pinecones

large mittens or boxing gloves

broom

top hat

On a flat even clearing, turn the garbage can upside down and press it into the snow to hold it in place. Using the shovel, mass and pack the snow up around the can until it is fully covered, and the snow is at least 1 foot thick on all sides. Spray snow with water and smooth as you go along, packing outward to round the form. Frosty's base should be approximately 3 feet high and approximately the same diameter. Push the 2-foot wooden stake into the top of the base, leaving at least 1 foot of the stake exposed.

To make Frosty's torso, roll a snowball $2\frac{1}{2}$ feet in diameter and place it on the exposed stake, or mass and pack a snowball directly on the base and around the stake. Roll another ball for the head, this time making a ball approximately $1\frac{1}{2}$ feet in diameter. Place the head on the torso ball and behold the classic three-ball snowman shape.

continued

Using the spoon, carve out holes for the eyes and insert the coal lumps. Push a wooden skewer into the fat end of the carrot and poke it in for the nose. Using toothpicks, peg the curved twig on the face for the mouth or give Frosty the traditional 6-rock smile. Give him a pipe, twist the scarf around the neck, and line his front with the pinecones for buttons. Attach the mittens or gloves with wooden skewers and tuck the broom into one of the gloves. Poke a small branch or stake into Frosty's head and hang his hat (watch him come alive and start singing).

note:

To make Frosty's rustic broom, you'll need a thick stick or pole approximately 4 feet long, a bundle of about 20 slender twigs or branches each approximately 2½ feet long, and 2 pieces of wire each approximately 1 foot long. Arrange the thin sticks around the bottom 6 inches of the stick. Hold the bundle with one hand and make one wire twist near the top of the broom head. Use the second wire to make another twist 4 inches below the first one. It is best to make the first twist by hand to hold the sticks in place, then turn with pliers to tighten the sticks. Trim off the loose wire ends.

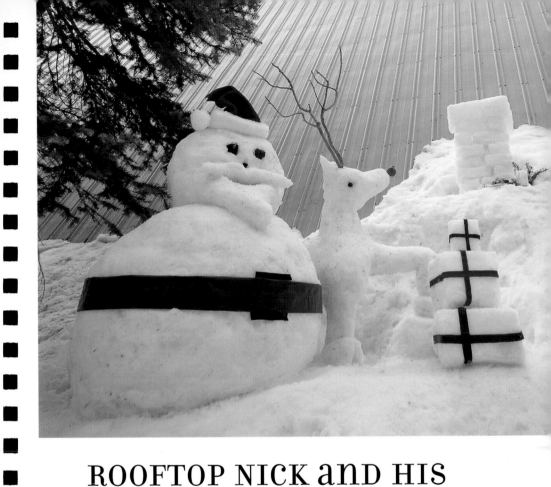

ROOFTOP NICK and HIS RED-NOSED SIDEKICK

THIS SANTA MIGHT BE too wide to fit down that chimney, but Rudolph still eagerly guides the way. We built Santa on a shelf carved into a snowbank sloping off the neighbor's roof and constructed a wood frame for Rudolph. You only need to make the front end of a frame—the two front legs and the head attached to a horizontal body. You can use pine or any other soft wood. If the frame seems like trouble, you can make Santa solo.

continued

shovels and other carving tools

wooden stake, 16 inches long

2-by-2-inch pine board,
4 feet long

screwdriver

10 wood screws, each $2\frac{1}{2}$ inches
long

2-by-2-inch pine board,
3 feet long

two 2-by-2-inch pine boards,
each 2 feet long

2-by-2-inch pine board,
$\frac{1}{2}$ foot long

2-by-2-inch pine board,
6 inches long

spray bottle filled with water

2 small forked branches, for
antlers

spoon

2 lumps of coal

textured black fabric such
as vinyl or felt, 4 inches wide
by 6 feet long, for belt

wooden skewers

Santa hat

small red apple

Build Santa in front of a snow-bank. Roll a snowball approximately 4 feet in diameter for Santa's base. Push the 16-inch stake into the base, leaving at least 12 inches exposed. Roll another snowball approximately 2 feet in diameter for Santa's head, and add it to the body. Smooth and round the form.

Now make Rudolph's frame:

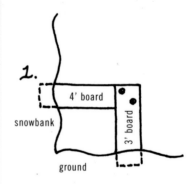

Using the screwdriver and 2 screws, attach the 4-foot pine board to the 3-foot board at a right angle. The longer piece is the torso, and the shorter piece is a straight leg. Hold the torso horizontally so that the leg touches the ground. Push the back end of the torso into the snowbank behind Santa. Push the leg into the ground.

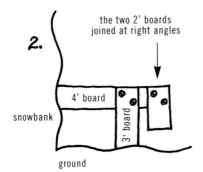

2.

the two 2' boards
joined at right angles

4' board

snowbank

3' board

ground

Using the screwdriver and 2 screws, attach one 2-foot board to the other 2-foot board at a right angle to make a second, bent leg. Using 2 screws, attach the bent leg to the straight leg at a right angle.

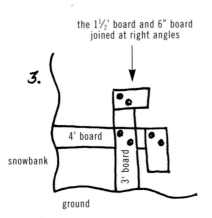

3.

the 1½' board and 6" board
joined at right angles

4' board

snowbank

3' board

ground

Using the screwdriver and 2 screws, attach the 1½-foot board

to the 6-inch board at a right angle. The longer piece is the neck, and the shorter piece is the head. Using the last 2 screws, attach this structure to the torso.

Spray the frame with water and pack it with snow. Continue to pack and spray until the snow is 6 inches thick around the frame. At the top of the head insert the branches for antlers. Pack and shape 2 ears and press them onto the head.

To decorate Santa and Rudolph, carve out holes for the eyes and insert the coal lumps. Pack and shape additional snow to make Santa's beard. Wrap the fabric around Santa's girth and secure with wooden skewers. Top Santa's head with his hat. Attach the apple with skewers for Rudolph's red nose.

1.

celebrity snowmen

INVITE YOUR FRIENDS TO a star-studded party on the front lawn. Ooh and aah as famous rock stars, artists, socialites, and mythological creatures pose for the paparazzi. If they give you the cold shoulder, don't worry—they'll melt before they wear out their welcome.

Basic Snow Head

To make a basic snow head, roll or carve a snowball approximately 1 foot in diameter. Insert a 16-inch stake into the base of the ball, leaving approximately two-thirds of the stake exposed. Insert the stake into a snowbank and shape the snow around it to form the neck. Smooth the face before you add features and decorations.

Snow people are fashion conscious. As Coco Chanel once said, "Adornment is never anything but a reflection of the self." Whatever, as far as we're concerned, the more accessories the better.

2.

3.

4.

Jackie Snow

KNOWN FOR HER PARED-DOWN elegance, Jackie remains one of the modern era's foremost fashion icons. To recreate her classic face, begin by shaping the Basic Snow Head into an oval. Pinch a tiny snowball into a triangle approximately 2 inches long and press into the face for the nose. To make the mouth, cut a tomato into 4 wedges. Scrape off the interior pulp from one of the wedges. Lay the resulting skin flat and cut out a thin opening. Use toothpicks to peg the lips to the face. Tie a kerchief around the head and add her signature glasses. Voilà Jacqueline!

Snow Punk

AS JOHNNY ROTTEN ONCE said, "There's no future! For this snowman!" Lay 6 carrots on a cutting board and trim the fat ends. Insert a wooden skewer firmly into the fat end of each carrot, leaving some of the skewer exposed. Insert the skewered carrots into the head in a row to make the mohawk. To make the ears, skewer 2 dried apricots on the diagonal into the sides of the face. Carve holes for the eyes and mouth, and press in marble eyes and the candy-corn teeth. Give Snow Punk a pine-needle nose-piercing.

PicasSnow

PicasSnow is thought to be the forefather of ice cubism so you can leave his head slightly square. For his nose and mouth, use long, wooden skewers to attach half of a butternut squash. Insert marbles or beads for eyes (you can put them both on one side, as was his style). Insert chile peppers and lettuce for ears. Fashion the hair with a leaf of kale and secure with a hat or beret filled with snow. A thin Japanese eggplant makes a bold eyebrow. You can add a shake or two of dry nontoxic tempera paint to re-create his famous blue period.

MeduSnow

Medusa's chilly gaze turned people to stone; MeduSnow's will turn you to ice. For the serpent hair, we used clusters of Chinese long beans, but you can substitute long licorice whips. Scoop out the top of her head and fill the hole with the bean clusters or licorice whips. Cover and pack with snow. Carve a mouth from an apple wedge and attach with skewers. Press in the tip of a fresh green pepper or chile for the nose. If you don't have mirror eyes, use colored marbles. Spike icicles and other jagged chunks of snow around her neck for added danger.

25

white-water kayaker

2 wooden stakes, each 16 inches long

2 slender sticks, each approximately 5 feet long

spoon

2 lumps of coal

plastic bottle cap

2 slender sticks, each approximately 4 inches long

hat

❄

Mass and pack a large rectangle of snow for the kayak approximately 2 feet wide by 2 feet high by 6 feet long. Insert one of the wooden stakes into the middle of the boat, leaving the top half of the stake exposed.

To make the body, roll a snowball approximately 2 feet in diameter and place it on the stake. Roll a second snowball, approximately 1 foot in diameter, and place it on top for the head.

Lay the second wooden stake across the rim of the boat and cover it with snow. To make the oars, attach the two 5-foot sticks by inserting them under the snow-covered stake. Now that you have completed the figure, carve the hull of the boat by shaving off each end to a point.

Using the spoon, carve out the eyes and insert the coal lumps. Press in the bottle-cap nose, and add the slender sticks for the mouth. Top with a hat and she's ready to row!

SHE'S A MIGHTY POWERFUL Snow Queen. Make her the queen of your dreams. Adorn her for Valentine's Day and make the Queen of Hearts. Add a passel of dwarves, some more hair, and she's Snow White.

snow queen

scissors

5 pieces felt in assorted colors (red, pink, brown, yellow, blue, or green)

thin cardboard, 8½ by 11 inches

white glue or staples

paintbrush

glitter

wooden skewers

2 yards flowing fabric such as rayon, polyester, or cotton

To make the felt decorations, cut almond shapes for eyes, pink circles for cheeks, and a heart shape for the mouth. Cut a strip of fringe for the hair and two smaller strips of fringe for the eyelashes. Trace and cut felt flower shapes at least 4 inches in diameter. (For more dynamic flowers, stack and glue a few flowers of various sizes on top of one another.)

To make the princess hat, roll the cardboard into a cone and fasten with glue or staples. Using scissors, trim excess paper from the base of the cone. Using the paintbrush, coat the outside of the cone with an even coat of glue and generously sprinkle with glitter. Allow to dry completely. To add glitter circles or stars, use a paintbrush to paint glue shapes and sprinkle with a second coat of glitter.

To make the body, mass and pack a conical mound approximately 5 feet high by 4 feet wide at the bottom. Flatten off the top of the form. (You should behold a Christmas tree shape with the tip cut off.) To make the head, roll a snowball approximately 1 foot in diameter and place it on the body. Pack snow around the neck to secure the head.

To initiate her reign, skewer the fabric behind her shoulders to make the royal cape. (If the wind is blowing hard, hold down the train with heavy snow chunks.) Press on the sovereign flower ornaments and crown her with the glitter cap.

If you've made your Snow Queen near the house, put a spotlight on her at night and watch her rule the dark universe.

note:

Add wings and a wide smile and she becomes an Ice Fairy. Add a wand and she's the Ice Fairy's godmother.

snow angel

shovel

heavy-duty flashlight with 12-volt batteries, preferably waterproof

10 thin wooden stakes or sticks, each approximately 2 feet long

aluminum or steel window screen, approximately 2 feet square

spray bottle filled with water

glue gun or baling wire

15 to 20 thin branches, each approximately 12 inches long

Find a flat, wide space for your angel. Dig a hole approximately 1 foot wide and 1 foot deep. Turn the flashlight on and place it, face up, in the hole. Lay the stakes across the hole to provide horizontal support for the screen. Place the wire screen over the stakes, centering it to cover the hole. Secure the screen, packing snow around the edges.

Roll a series of snowballs each 5 inches in diameter, and place them in a ring around the edge of the hole. Pack them tightly so they touch. Spray with water to freeze and solidify the form. On top of the ring, stack a second layer of snowballs, this time using one less ball to make the form slope slightly inward. Repeat the process until you have a snowball tower in the shape of a cone. Roll the top ball slightly larger for the head.

Just as George helped Clarence earn his wings in *It's a Wonderful Life*, help your Snow Angel earn hers. To make each wing, glue or wire 2 thin branches together at a 120-degree angle. Add the remaining sticks, fanning them out and wiring or gluing as you go along. Carefully poke the finished wings into the snow behind your angel.

CHAPTER TWO

creatures OF THE snow

SNOW BUDDY

WHO DO YOU CALL when you run out of snowballs? Snow Buddy!
Snow buddy goes where you go with his red wagon and cross-
county skis. You can buy a miniature wagon at a toy store and
dress your buddy with any large doll or baby clothes. An upside-
down measuring cup makes a perfect hat. Wooden spatulas make
great snowshoes.

SNOWBUGS, ALSO KNOWN AS Lady Snowbird Beetles, make a beautiful sight in a barren winter garden. While the master snow carver whittles away at the form, kids can mix up a rainbow of spots (recipe follows) or decorate with bright buttons, felt rounds, pushpins, or gumdrops.

snowbugs on a log

carving tools such as serrated knife or a spatula

wooden skewer

8 long pine needles

24 thin crooked sticks, each approximately 4 inches long

raisins

Snow Spots (directions follow) or other round decorations such as felt rounds, buttons, and colored pushpins

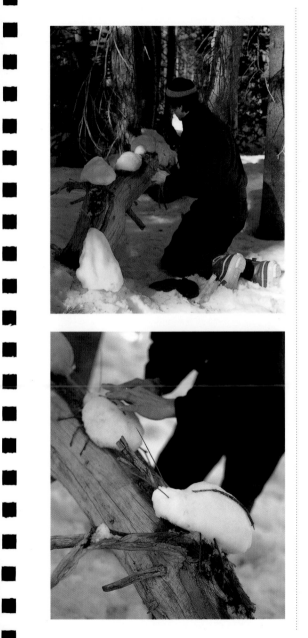

Roll or carve 4 separate snow-balls each approximately 1 foot in diameter. Place the balls in a line along the ground or atop a log or fallen tree. Shape each ball into a rounded football, using the scrapings to form heads. Use a wooden skewer to poke 2 holes at the top of each head. Insert pine needles into each hole for antennae. Insert 6 sticks under each bug body, 3 on each side, for the legs. Depending on your terrain, you can angle the legs in various positions to make the bugs look like they're crawling.

Press in the raisins for eyes. Decorate the bugs with snow spots (directions follow) or other materials. The addition of a curved stick laid lengthwise suggests the bug's wings.

MIX UP THESE SPOTS outside. If they melt, you can make creepy oozing monster beetles. If you don't have a circular cookie cutter, use the rim of a glass to cut the spots.

snow spots

mixing bowls (one for each different color)

spoons (one for each bowl)

nontoxic dry tempera paint in the color or colors of your choice

cookie sheets

1-inch round cookie cutter

Fill each mixing bowl with 4 cups of snow. Add 2 tablespoons tempera paint to each bowl and stir to make a paste. Spread each mixture onto a separate cookie sheet, pressing down to make smooth, flat "snowdough" approximately half an inch thick. Using the cookie cutter, cut out the spots. (At this point you can take your spots inside and freeze them for future use.) Using a spatula, slide the spots onto each bug and press into place.

WHEN IT'S SNOWING TOO hard for the bunny slope, make a few on your porch. Here, Flopsy and Mopsy hop on all fours, but you can make the white rabbit on two legs and give him a pocket watch so he won't be late.

snow Bunnies

stick or spoon (optional)

toothpicks

pennies

❄

Roll a snowball approximately 1 foot in diameter for the body. Roll a second snowball approximately half the size of the first ball. Place it on or just in front of the body. Pack snow around the neck. Using your hands, roll out 2 long snow ears and plant them on the top of the head. If necessary, shape the ears with a stick or a spoon. Insert toothpick whiskers, 3 to each side, and press in 2 pennies for eyes. A tiny snowball on the back makes the tail. Put the tail high for an alert bunny, low for a sleepy bunny. Repeat and watch them multiply.

WHEN PORCUPINENEEDLES ARE STARTLED, their quills stand straight up. Perhaps this one saw the dog and cat around the corner. If the quills startle you, layer leaves instead of pine needles to make an armadillo.

porcupineneeдle

screwdriver

pine needle clusters

5 pinecones

2 almonds

1 branch with leaves or pine needles attached

To make the body, roll a snowball approximately 3 feet long by 2 feet round. Smooth the ball into an oval. Roll a smaller ball approximately one-third the size of the first and attach it to the front end of the body. Using the screwdriver, poke 2-inch-deep holes in rows across the length of the figure. Insert a cluster of pine needles into each hole. The closer you space the holes, the thicker the fur will be. (For the porcupineneedle pictured here, the clusters are spaced approximately 1 inch apart.) Press in 4 of the pinecones for feet, then press in the final cone for the nose. Press in the almond eyes, and lay the branch at the back for the tail.

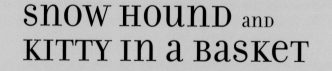

SNOW HOUND and
KITTY IN a BaSKET

instructions for
KITTY IN a BaSKET
begin on page 42

THIS LONG-BODIED, SHORT-LEGGED SNOW hound was once the national dog of the Teutonic Empire.

snow hound

1 wooden stake, $2\frac{1}{2}$ feet long

spray bottle filled with water

1 stick, 16 inches long

carving tools

1 eggplant, halved

wooden skewers

2 pebbles or lumps of coal

1 small pinecone

Roll 2 large snowballs each approximately 2 feet in diameter. Place them 2 feet apart. Lay the wooden stake across them, and firmly attach the ends to each snowball, packing and pressing snow on top. Spray the stake with water and pack with more snow. Your dog should now resemble a snow-covered barbell.

Poke the 16-inch stick into one end of the form leaving half of it exposed, and pack snow around it to make the neck. For the head, roll another snowball approximately 1 foot in diameter and attach it to the neck. Carve the head and snout.

Carve tunnels through each base snowball to form legs. Skewer each eggplant half to the head for the ears. Press in pebbles for eyes, and insert the tip of a pinecone for the nose. An additional stick in the back makes a wagging tail.

THIS KITTY IS TOO cold to cuddle, but she loves to curl up in her basket. The basket itself is simple to make, and if the cat runs away, you can use it for other projects. Fill it with flowers for an entryway bouquet or call it a corral and hold a winter rodeo.

KITTY In a Basket

15 thick sticks, each at least 1 foot long

hammer (optional)

approximately 40 thin twigs, each at least 6 inches long

garden shears

2 almonds

pebble

6 pipe cleaners

To make the basket, make a circle with the 15 sticks, hammering or pressing them into the ground approximately 6 inches apart. Weave the twigs horizontally in and out between the vertical sticks to create the basket sides. Using the garden shears, trim off the vertical stakes and any other loose ends.

To make the kitty, roll a snowball approximately $1\frac{1}{2}$ feet in diameter and place it in the basket. Roll a second ball approximately 1 foot in diameter and place it on the body. Pack snow around the neck. Cut out a V-shaped wedge from the top of the head, leaving 2 peaks for ears. Insert the almonds for eyes and the pebble for a nose. Insert the pipe cleaners, 3 to each side, for the kitty's trembling whiskers.

NO DANGER HERE, WILL ROBINSON! Make this classic snowbot or design your own. Give him 6 legs, 4 arms, 2 heads, or wheels. How many heads does that thing have?

snowbot

square plastic storage container, approximately 6 inches square by 2½ inches deep

rectangular plastic storage container, approximately 5 by 4 by 2 inches

kitchen knife

empty half-gallon milk carton with the top cut off

2 red pushpins

2 screws

❄

To make the base, mold snow in the square container. Unmold by inverting the container. Repeat, stacking the second mold on top of the first, building a base approximately 5 inches high. To make the feet, mold snow in the rectangular container. Unmold the block and cut it in half using the kitchen knife. Place the halves at the front of the base. To make the torso, mold snow in the milk carton. Unmold the snow onto the base. To make the arms and the head, mold five more blocks in the rectangular container. Stack two on each side for the arms and place one on top of the torso.

To decorate snowbot's face, press in the pushpins for the eyes and the screws for the mouth.

THAR SHE BLOWS! SNOWBY, the frosty white whale, still lives in the swell of his more famous cousin. We built our 20-foot Snowby into an existing snowbank with a rounded hump. This is a great all-day project for the whole family, and after all that work, you can turn Snowby into Stega-snow-rus the following day (see page 47).

SNOWBY DICK

shovels

hammer

2 branches or stakes, each
   approximately 3 feet long

spray bottle filled with water

carving tools

garden trowel

large pot lid

❄

Using a team of people and many shovels, shore up or mass the snow into an enormous oval mound approximately 16 feet long and 7 feet high at the peak, tapering to a tail at waist height (approximately 2 feet).

In the tail end, hammer the two branches into the tail end in a V shape. Spray the branches with water. Pack snow around the branches, spraying as you work, until each stick is approximately 2 feet thick with snow. At this point you should have a rough forked tail that you can shape into flat flukes using your carving tools.

Once you have the basic mass, square off the contours with a shovel. Smooth and round the top, front, and sides of the whale. Give him definition with a deep undercut in the ground along the entire length of the form. The resulting shadows will make Snowby appear to ride the waves.

Scoop out the mouth with the garden trowel. Cut snow blocks or icicles for teeth. Press in the pot lid for the eye. Carve a fort in his belly and crawl inside like Jonah.

AFTER YOU'VE WORKED LONG and hard to make Snowby Dick, you can rearrange him the next day to make a Stega-snow-rus, one of the few dinosaurs to survive the Ice Age.

stega-snow-rus

shovels

carving tools

empty half-gallon milk carton with the top cut off (optional)

2 brightly colored coffee or measuring cups

Carve the snow away from Snowby's tail and remove the sticks. Move the excess snow sideways and around, packing it to form the dinosaur tail. Remove the pot lid eye and fill in Snowby's mouth and eyes with snow. You will now have a round mass approximately 7 feet tall by 18 feet long, with a long, curving tail.

On each side, approximately one third of the way in from the front and back, add arms and legs by massing and packing four mounds each approximately 3 feet high by $1\frac{1}{2}$ feet wide. At the front of these mounds, add forearms and forelegs by massing and

packing additional snow mounds, each approximately 1 foot high by 2 feet long. Firmly pack the mounds, and we mean hard! Use the carving tools to cut and shape the curving claws.

To make the head, mound an oblong snowball approximately 4 feet high by 2 feet long. Attach it to the front of the body, curving the mound slightly toward the tail. Carve the mouth, adding a tongue or teeth as you wish.

Form snow spikes with your hands, or use the milk carton as a mold. Line the spikes in rows down the dinosaur's back. To finish off the figure, use a shovel to make deep undercuts along the belly.

The addition of brightly colored coffee or measuring cups as eyes will bring your dinosaur to life.

As the dinosaur starts to melt, he'll turn your yard into a La Brea Snow Pit.

LET THE INVASION BEGIN.

ALIEN

shovel

carving tools

2 pinecones

2 small twigs

Using the shovel, mass and pack
a tall, firm mound approximately
3 feet high and 2 feet wide at
the base. Mark a point at which
the head will begin, one third of
the way down from the top of the
mound. Below that point, gently
shave away snow from both sides
of the mound to make a long,
creepy neck. Carve out holes in
the head and insert pinecone
eyes. Add the twigs to make the
nostrils. Suddenly you'll wish you
were somewhere else.

COULD THIS BE ROSWELL revisited or just a snow encounter of the third kind? Create your very own Area 51 right in the backyard.

snow encounters

shovel

carving tools

battery-powered Christmas lights

teacup

To make the space ship, mass a mound of snow 6 feet long by 5 feet high (or find an existing snow mound of this size). Using the shovel, make vertical cuts around the mound to square it off. Clear away the excess snow from around the base. Round and smooth the top and dig a deep undercut along the contour of the base. Dig a deeper trench on one side of the ship, and shave off the underbelly to lift the nose slightly off the ground. This will make the ship look like it has just landed.

Carve a thin channel, 1 inch wide by 2 inches deep, around the top of the ship. Lay in the Christmas lights. Carefully pack the snow in and around the cords. Add interstellar warts using the teacup as a mold. (The warts are proven to reduce intergalactic white noise by 36 percent.)

winter palace

THE MASSIVE RESIDENCES OF royalty took centuries to build, but this miniature castle takes only minutes to make. Design your own royal fortress. Build the foundation on a rock for Edinburgh castle. Use a plastic coffee filter to make conical turrets for mad King Ludwig's Neuschwanstein (the inspiration for the familiar blue Disney castle). Cup large rounded shapes to make the Taj Mahal.

ice-cube storage box or other
   large square plastic container

8-inch cake pan

plastic half-gallon pitcher

coffee cup or bowl

12 ice cubes

carving tools

To make the walls, mold snow in the ice-cube storage box. Unmold by inverting the box. Repeat until you have 4 walls. Place the walls, corner to corner, in the shape of a square fortress. To make column bases, mold snow in the cake pan. Unmold and repeat until you have 4 circular bases. Place one base at each corner of the fortress. To make the towers, mold snow in the pitcher. Unmold and repeat until you have 4 towers. Place one tower on top of each base. To make turrets, mold snow in the coffee cup. Unmold and repeat until you have 4 turrets. Place one turret on each of the four towers.

Crenellate the walls with ice cubes. Carve the windows and doors and dig a miniature moat to keep out snow aliens.

AND YOU THOUGHT YOU'D have to fly to Bermuda to golf in the winter. With Snow Green, tee off year-round and leave your three-put reputation behind!

snow green

scissors

thin piece of cardboard, approximately 4 by 6 inches

felt in color of choice, approximately 4 by 6 inches

pencil

white glue

clear tape

broomstick or other thin pole

empty large soup or coffee can

spoon

To make the flag, use the scissors to cut the cardboard in half on the diagonal. Place 1 triangle on one corner of the felt. Using the pencil, trace the triangle. Move the triangle to the opposite corner of the felt and trace again. Cut out the felt triangles and glue them to each side of the cardboard triangle. Tape the flag to the broomstick and set aside.

Stake out a wide plot of snow at least 15 feet long by 8 feet wide. (You may want to pack the snow with a board, but feel free to let nature's obstacles challenge your game.) At one end of the plot, use the can to mark the size and spot for your hole. Using the spoon, dig a hole as deep as the can is tall. Insert the can into the hole, open end up, and plant the pole beside the can. Listen for the satisfying clunk as you sink your shot.

AFTER THE PLOWS CLEAR the streets, the resulting snowbanks are perfect for making outdoor hearths. Smooth off the sides of your hearth for the clean modern look or leave them craggy for a cave effect. The ideal bank is at least 5 feet tall and of firmly packed snow. We lit 50 tea light candles, but a few tall votive candles should provide quite a glow. Be sure to put your candles in holders so they don't blow out.

Arctic Hearth

shovel

flat scrapers

carving tools

50 tea light or 10 tall votive candles with candle holders

1 long-handled kitchen lighter

If the snowbank does not have a smooth, flat face at least 5 feet wide, square it off by making long vertical cuts with the shovel. In the face of the bank, beginning 2 feet off the ground, dig a rough rectangular hole 4 feet wide by 3 feet tall by 2 feet deep. Using flat scrapers, scrape the bottom of the hearth flat. Square off the back wall and the sides. Fill your hearth with tea lights and votive candles. Using the long-handled kitchen lighter, light the candles from back to front.

To turn your hearth into a brick fireplace, cut 2 columns, each approximately 1 foot wide and 6 inches deep on each side of your hearth. Cut snow slabs, each approximately 3 inches thick, from another part of the snowbank, and stack them in the column hollows to form pillars on each side of the hearth. (Cut the slabs smooth like bricks or rough like flagstones—very popular these days!)

note:

Don't leave the burning hearth unattended.

← seven
FOOT
FR❋STY!

THIS SNOWMOBILE COMES COMPLETE with four-wheel drive, and you can park this compact in any garage. Use this same technique to create trucks, vans, semis, cement mixers, even a Caterpillar tractor. Carve out streets and get ready for a traffic jam.

snowmobile

standard shoebox or other
   rectangular container

long knife

sheet of blue cellophane or a
   blue plastic bag

scissors

4 bottle caps

2 toothpicks or pine needles

2 dimes

Mold snow in the shoebox. Unmold by inverting the shoebox. Repeat to create a second block. Cut 1 block in half crosswise and center 1 half atop the uncut block. You can move the half forward to make a truck or backward to make a Cadillac. To make wheels, roll four small snowballs and press them against the car body, hollowing out wheel wells if desired. Accessorize the car with windows cut from the cellophane or plastic bag, bottle-cap hubcaps, toothpick or pine needle windshield wipers, and headlights made with dimes.

DRAFT THE BEST SNOWBALL thrower to be on your team and build your ramparts as high as you can. We molded our blocks using plastic recycling containers. Cardboard boxes will work in a pinch, but they'll become soggy and won't last if you plan on building the Great Wall of China.

snow FORT

large square plastic containers such as coolers or mail or storage boxes

Mold snow in the containers. Be sure to fill the them completely, including the corners. Pack down the snow tightly. Unmold the block by inverting the container. Mold at least 8 blocks for the base of the wall and stack blocks upward, overlapping the spaces between them. Repeat until the wall reaches the desired height. Use the empty containers as an armory; store up snowballs and then attack. A flag is useful to identify the enemy if you are battling in a blizzard (see Snow Green, page 56).

snow on the Range

PLAYING IN THE SNOW is all about letting your imagination run wild. This good old boy is a result of one such snow flurry of creativity. We haven't included a recipe for our favorite cowpoke, because we know he's a little out there, but you might find inspiration in his carefree attitude. Un-lasso the wacky, snow-roaming spirit and see where it takes you. Happy trails!

CHAPTER FOUR

no-snow snowmen

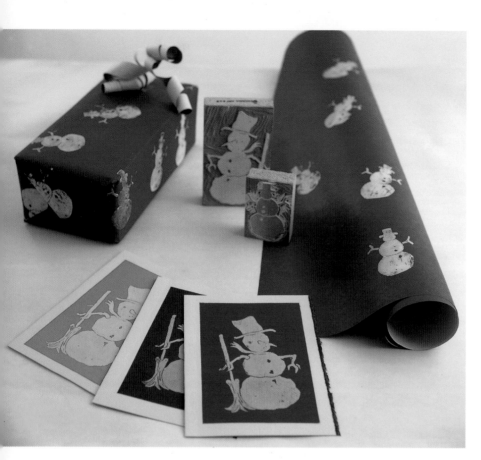

snowman prints

USE THESE TWO SIMPLE techniques to make an array of cards and wrapping papers. While adults might enjoy whittling away on the linoleum blocks, the no-carve potato prints are great for kids.

IN THIS SIMPLE PRINTING technique, 3 vertical stamps using a potato half make the essential snowman shape. Draw in the details with markers or crayons.

STACKED POTATO PRINTS

small potato, cut in half crosswise

paintbrush

white water-soluble ink or acrylic paint

assorted colored papers

colored pens or crayons

To make the snowman shape, brush 1 potato half with white paint and press it onto a piece of colored paper. Remove and repeat twice, making 3 prints in a row. Allow to dry thoroughly. Use the pens or crayons to draw in the eyes, nose, mouth, arms, and scarf. Don't forget the top hat!

BE ESPECIALLY CAREFUL WHEN carving with the linoleum cutter. It is very sharp!

LINOLEUM BLOCK PRINTS

linoleum block

pencil

linoleum cutter

white water-soluble ink or acrylic paint

ink roller or paintbrush

assorted colored papers

Use the pencil to outline a snow-man directly on the block. When you have the design you like, use the linoleum cutter to remove the linoleum outside the edges of your drawing, leaving a positive image. Make sure you cut away from yourself and from others!

Once you have carved your block, brush or roll the paint evenly over the uncut linoleum. Press the block onto the colored paper and remove to reveal a snowman print. Allow to dry thoroughly before using.

MAKE A QUICK AND easy greeting card with a color copy of your favorite snow creation. The quality of the image will depend on the copier. We made a color copy of a black-and-white photo to give the image vintage appeal. Or bypass the copier altogether and make a limited-edition card by mounting the original photograph.

keepsake cards

copy of a favorite photograph, approximately 3 inches by 4 inches

colored paper sheet, approximately 4 inches by 5 inches

glue stick

blank card, approximately 5 inches by 6 inches, with matching envelope

Trim any excess paper away from the image, making sure the edges are straight. Center and glue the photocopied image onto the colored paper. Center and glue the colored paper onto the blank card. Allow to dry. Scribble your message and send it off. Won't grandma be impressed!

THIS PUDGY STOCKING IS made of felt and stitched with a sewing machine, although you can also sew it by hand. Fill Frosty with oodles of presents. To make a hefty bean bag, stuff him with beans or rice and stitch him closed.

FROSTY'S STOCKING

2 sheets of typing paper, each 8½ by 11 inches

scotch tape

pencil

scissors

2 pieces white felt, each 10 by 15 inches

sewing pins

decorations, such as colored felt, buttons, beads, sticks

Tape the sheets of paper together side by side. Use the pencil to sketch a basic Frosty shape using the full length of the taped sheets. To do this, draw 3 overlapping ovals. The bottom oval should be approximately 8 inches wide by 6½ inches tall, the center oval approximately 6 inches wide by 5 inches tall, and the head approximately 5 inches wide by 4 inches tall. Overlap each oval 1 full inch. Frosty's neck should be at least

$3\frac{1}{2}$ inches wide. Using the scissors, cut out the pattern.

Stack the 2 pieces of white felt and pin the Frosty pattern to them. Cut out the shape. Unpin and remove the pattern. Pin the 2 felt snowmen back together. Sew the 2 pieces of felt together, stitching $\frac{1}{2}$ inch in from the edge. At the top of the head, leave a 2-inch unsewn gap. (This is the opening for the stocking stuffers.) On the back of Frosty's head, carefully snip a $\frac{1}{2}$-inch horizontal slit in the center of the back felt, approximately 2 inches down from the top. This will allow you to hang Frosty.

Decorate Frosty any way you like. We stitched a jaunty cap out of black felt. Then we hand-stitched buttons onto his front to make his coat. His eyes and mouth are beads, and his mouth is a string of tiny beads. For his carrot nose, we cut a narrow triangle of orange felt approximately 1 inch tall and $\frac{1}{2}$ inch wide, folded it in half and stitched the fold together. A few more stitches attached the "carrot" to his face. We finished Frosty with stick arms stitched behind the side seams at "shoulder" level.

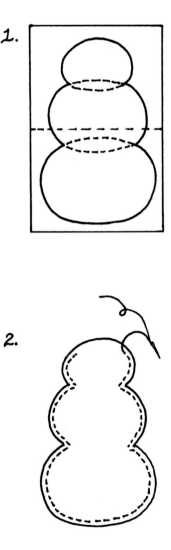

1.

2.

SHREDDED COCONUT MAKES THESE snowmen especially flaky. We baked the macaroons in three sizes of metal measuring cups, but you can use a set of three round cookie cutters in descending sizes. MAKES 2 MEN

macaroon men

4 egg whites

1 cup granulated sugar

1 teaspoon vanilla extract

1 teaspoon ground cinnamon

1 tablespoon honey

$1\frac{1}{4}$ cups sifted cake flour

2 cups (8 ounces) shredded
    dried coconut

confectioners' sugar

4 cinnamon sticks

4 whole cloves

In a heatproof bowl, combine the egg whites, granulated sugar, vanilla, ground cinnamon and honey. Place over (not touching) barely simmering water in a saucepan and whisk until the sugar dissolves, approximately 2 minutes. Remove the bowl from the heat. Using a rubber spatula, fold in the flour and the coconut. Cover and refrigerate until well chilled, about 2 hours or as long as overnight.

Preheat the oven to 350° F.

Grease 2 sets of 3 metal measuring cups in descending sizes— $\frac{1}{2}$ cup, $\frac{1}{4}$ cup, and $\frac{1}{8}$ cup—or round cookie cutters in descending sizes with a 3-inch cookie cutter for the base. Fill each cup not more than three-fourths full. Place the measuring cup on a greased baking sheet. Bake until light brown. The smaller-sized macaroons will take approximately 30 minutes, while the larger sizes will take up to 45 minutes. Transfer to a rack to cool.

When cool, gently remove each macaroon ball. Stack each set, largest to smallest, on a plate. Dust with confectioners' sugar. Insert cinnamon sticks for arms and poke in the cloves for eyes.

marshmallow men

WHEN DIPPED IN HOT cocoa, these white chocolate marshmallow men melt into a creamy froth. For a quick and easy version, leave out the chocolate and just stack mini marshmallows onto toothpicks.
MAKES 4 MARSHMALLOW MEN

$\frac{1}{2}$ cup confectioners' sugar

8 large marshmallows

1 bar (8-ounces) white chocolate

❄

Spread the confectioners' sugar onto a plate.

Microwave the marshmallows on high for 30 seconds to melt fully. Using a greased spoon, stir until smooth. Using 2 greased teaspoons, shape the mixture into 12 balls. Drop each ball into the powdered sugar and roll to coat. Set the balls aside and allow to cool.

In a small bowl, microwave the chocolate on high for 30 seconds to melt fully. Stir until smooth. With a knife, spread a teaspoonful of the chocolate over the surface of 1 marshmallow ball. Set the ball on a cookie sheet. Spread another marshmallow ball with chocolate and place it next to the first, gently pressing the marsh-mallow balls together. Repeat once more to create the classic three-snowball shape. Continue with the remaining marshmallows and chocolate to make four marshmallow men.

Float your marshmallow men in cups of hot cocoa and watch them melt.

WITH THREE SCOOPS OF ice cream set in a cone, you can make a truly tasty snowman. Set out a tray of colorful candies and toothsome treats and let everyone decorate their own creation. Eat him fast before he melts!

ice cream man

ice cream

cone

gumdrops for hats

raisins for eyes

mini M&M's for buttons

2 Twix sticks for arms

Licorice for mouth

Fruit leather or 2 sour strips
   for scarves

Scoop and pack three balls of ice cream into the cone. Decorate with gumdrops, raisins, mini M&M's, Twix sticks, licorice whips, and fruit leather. Eat. Enjoy.

meringue man

MERINGUE MAN MAKES A lovely centerpiece. Admire him through dinner before pulling off his head for dessert! You can trace plates to make the pattern. Use a 6-inch plate for the base, a 4-inch plate for the middle, and a 3-inch plate for the head. Make the top head tall. MAKES 1 MAN

8 egg whites

2 cups granulated sugar

1 teaspoon cream of tartar

candy decorations such as red
hots or jelly beans

2 cinnamon sticks

confectioners' sugar

Preheat the oven to 175° F.

Lay a 14-inch long piece of
parchment on a flat work surface.
Using a pencil, draw a snowman
pattern (see headnote). Place the
parchment paper pattern-side
down on a large baking sheet.
You should still be able to read
the pattern.

In a heatproof bowl, combine the
egg whites, granulated sugar,
and cream of tartar. Place over
(not touching) barely simmering
water in a saucepan and whisk
until the sugar dissolves, approximately 2 minutes.

Remove the bowl from over the
heat. Using an electric mixer,
set on high speed, beat the egg
whites until stiff peaks form,
10 to 12 minutes.

Fill a pastry bag (with a $\frac{1}{2}$-inch
opening) with meringue. Pipe
meringue onto the parchment
paper, tracing the outlines of the
3 circles. Fill each circle by pip-
ing the meringue in smaller and
smaller concentric circles. You
should have 3 touching circles.

Bake until firm but not hard, about
15 minutes. Remove from the oven
and add the candy decorations,
making the eyes, nose, mouth and
buttons. Return to the oven and
bake until firm, about 15 minutes
longer. Watch it carefully, and if it
starts to brown, remove it immedi-
ately. Add cinnamon stick arms
and dust with confectioners' sugar.
Place the baking sheet on a rack
and allow to cool completely.

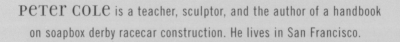

PETER COLE is a teacher, sculptor, and the author of a handbook on soapbox derby racecar construction. He lives in San Francisco.

FRANKIE FRANKENY is a San Francisco–based photographer whose work has appeared in numerous publications and books, including *The Art of Chocolate, Sorbets and Ice Creams, After-Dinner Drinks, Wraps*, and *The Star Wars Cookbook*.

LESLIE JONATH is an editor and writer living in San Francisco. She is the author of *Postmark Paris: A Little Album of Memories*.